DECOMPOSERS
Larvae

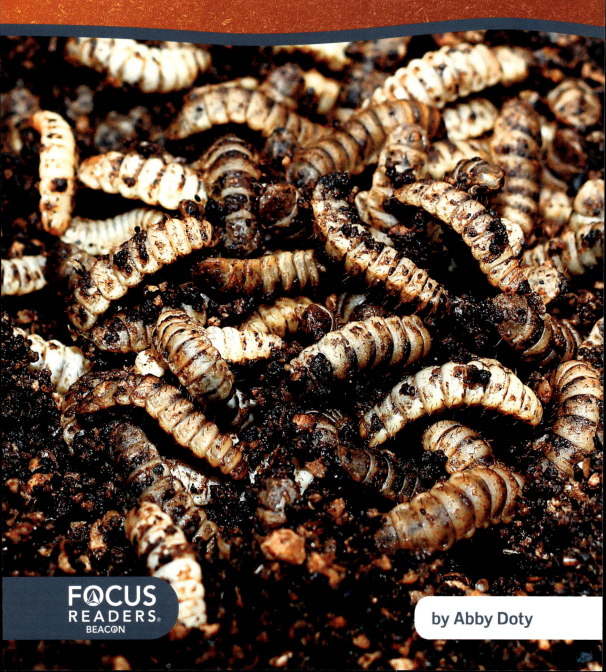

FOCUS READERS®
BEACON

by Abby Doty

www.focusreaders.com

Copyright © 2025 by Focus Readers®, Mendota Heights, MN 55120. All rights reserved. No part of this book may be reproduced or utilized in any form or by any means without written permission from the publisher.

Focus Readers is distributed by North Star Editions:
sales@northstareditions.com | 888-417-0195

Produced for Focus Readers by Red Line Editorial.

Photographs ©: Shutterstock Images, cover, 1, 6, 8, 11, 13, 14, 17, 18, 20, 23, 25, 27, 29; iStockphoto, 4

Library of Congress Cataloging-in-Publication Data
Names: Doty, Abby, author.
Title: Larvae / Abby Doty.
Description: Mendota Heights, MN: Focus Readers, 2025. | Series: Decomposers | Includes index. | Audience: Grades 2-3
Identifiers: LCCN 2024035359 (print) | LCCN 2024035360 (ebook) | ISBN 9798889983996 (hardcover) | ISBN 9798889984276 (paperback) | ISBN 9798889984818 (pdf) | ISBN 9798889984559 (ebook)
Subjects: LCSH: Larvae--Juvenile literature.
Classification: LCC QL544.2 .D68 2025 (print) | LCC QL544.2 (ebook) | DDC 595.78--dc23/eng/20240830
LC record available at https://lccn.loc.gov/2024035359
LC ebook record available at https://lccn.loc.gov/2024035360

Printed in the United States of America
Mankato, MN
012025

About the Author

Abby Doty is a writer, editor, and booklover from Minnesota.

Table of Contents

CHAPTER 1
Feeding Time 5

CHAPTER 2
Flies and Beetles 9

CHAPTER 3
Spreading Nutrients 15

CHAPTER 4
Larvae Relationships 21

THAT'S AMAZING!
Losing Ecosystems 26

Focus Questions • 28
Glossary • 30
To Learn More • 31
Index • 32

CHAPTER 1
Feeding Time

A fly buzzes through the air. She is carrying lots of eggs. Then, she smells a dead fox. It is miles away. She starts flying toward it.

The fly soon arrives. She lays her many eggs across the fox's body.

 Flies can smell bodies from up to 10 miles (16 km) away.

Fly eggs are small. Flies lay the eggs in piles.

Over several days, the fly's eggs hatch. The **larvae** crawl out. Other fly larvae are already there. All of the larvae move as one across the fox. They begin eating.

Other insects come to feed, too. Eventually, the larvae become full. They move away from the fox's body. The larvae's skin becomes hard. These casings cover their bodies. The larvae become **pupae**. Later, they fly off as adults.

Did You Know?
Flies can lay hundreds of eggs at a time.

CHAPTER 2
Flies and Beetles

Ecosystems include three groups. Producers make their own food. Consumers eat plants or animals. And decomposers break down dead things to get energy. Some larvae are decomposers.

 More than 120,000 kinds of flies exist.

Larvae are the young forms of certain insects. For example, young flies are larvae. They are called maggots. Young beetles are larvae, too. They are called grubs. Larvae eventually become pupae. Then pupae become adult insects.

Larvae feed on several kinds of matter. Some larvae eat dying or dead plants. The larvae may shred dead leaves on the ground. Or they may tunnel into dying wood. Other larvae eat animal poop. Flies lay

Flies are larvae for only a few days. But beetles can be larvae for weeks, months, or even years.

eggs on the waste. Some beetles bring the poop to their tunnels. The grubs feed on it underground.

Other larvae feed on dead animals. Flies lay their eggs or larvae on the dead animal's body. Once maggots reach the food, they let out chemicals. The chemicals break down the body. Then the maggots can eat it.

Beetles arrive at bodies later. They lay their eggs or larvae on

Did You Know?
Beetles make up about 25 percent of all animal **species** on Earth.

 Grubs have strong mandibles. They can easily bite through roots and plants.

the dead body, too. Grubs use their **mandibles** to eat. Some beetles bury dead animals. Then, the grubs can feed on them safely, away from other animals.

CHAPTER 3
Spreading Nutrients

Larvae help ecosystems in several ways. They break down many dead things. For example, larvae eat leaf litter. This layer of dead plant parts covers the ground. Larvae break down dead animals, too.

 Large forests can drop tons of leaves each year.

Without decomposers, these things would pile up. So would animal waste.

Larvae help spread **nutrients**, too. Living plants have many nutrients in them. Nutrients help plants grow. And when plants grow, consumers have more food to eat. However, the nutrients stay inside plants and animals after they die. Most living things can't get those nutrients. That's where larvae come in. They help put the nutrients back into the

Larvae pass nutrients through their waste.

ecosystem. New plants can then use the nutrients to grow. Later, animals can get the nutrients by eating the plants.

When decomposing plants, larvae create a layer of humus on the soil.

Humus is a thick, dark substance.

Humus is broken-down leaf litter. It has many nutrients. Fungi and **bacteria** live in humus. They are both decomposers. They help pass on more nutrients that new plants can use.

Humus also helps make the soil richer. It lets air and water move easier through the dirt. As a result, plants grow better. Grubs can help soil, too. They often live and feed underground. They crawl through the dirt. This process mixes the soil's nutrients around. It also adds new nutrients.

Did You Know?
Tens of thousands of maggots may decompose a single dead animal or plant at the same time.

CHAPTER 4
Larvae Relationships

Larvae help return nutrients to the soil. However, larvae also interact with life-forms in other ways. For instance, fungi break down dead wood from the inside. This process creates holes that larvae can enter.

Larvae help add nitrogen and phosphorus to soil.

Next, the larvae break down the wood even more. That lets other life-forms feed on it. These animals include millipedes and worms. Also, larvae add moisture to the bodies of dead animals. That wetness helps bacteria access the body. Bacteria help break down bodies further.

Larvae also serve as food for other animals. For example, larvae may hatch on a dead animal's body. Soon, other insects will arrive. They include wasps, ants, and beetles.

Many birds eat larvae. Larvae can provide birds with more nutrients than other insects.

These predators feed on some of the larvae. When that happens, the insects get nutrients from the larvae. Later, larger animals come to eat. These animals often include squirrels, skunks, and raccoons.

In these ways, larvae help the entire ecosystem.

Larvae help humans, too. Farm animals create a lot of waste. Often, bacteria break down the waste. This process lets out many **greenhouse gases**. These gases are causing **climate change**. But larvae can

Did You Know?
Farms that raise animals create more than 11 percent of the world's greenhouse gases.

Some farmers use the larvae of black soldier flies to break down animal waste.

also break down animal waste. Compared to bacteria, larvae let out fewer harmful gases. Farmers can also use the larvae to feed farm animals. The larvae are full of protein, fats, and other nutrients.

THAT'S AMAZING!

Losing Ecosystems

Ecosystems need insect decomposers. For example, dung beetles help get rid of poop. Without them, the waste would stay on the ground. Waste can carry many diseases. It can cause humans and animals to get sick.

Many insect decomposers are decreasing in numbers. People often cut down natural areas. As a result, insects are losing their homes. Climate change also hurts insects and their larvae. Climate change can make places warmer. As temperatures rise, flies and beetles may spread to cooler areas. They could take over new ecosystems.

> Dung beetles eat and lay eggs in waste. Some dung beetles move large balls of waste.

Focus Questions

Write your answers on a separate piece of paper.

1. Write a few sentences explaining the main ideas of Chapter 3.
2. Would you want larvae living near you? Why or why not?
3. What do flies and beetles become after they are larvae?
   - **A.** humus
   - **B.** producers
   - **C.** pupae
4. Why might grubs need to eat away from other animals?
   - **A.** so other animals don't eat the grubs
   - **B.** so the grubs don't eat other larvae
   - **C.** so producers don't eat the grubs

5. What does **predators** mean in this book?

*Soon, other insects will arrive. They include wasps, ants, and beetles. These **predators** feed on some of the larvae.*

    A. animals that eat other animals
    B. animals that have six legs
    C. animals that dig underground

6. What does **diseases** mean in this book?

*Waste can carry many **diseases**. It can cause humans and animals to get sick.*

    A. leaves
    B. illnesses
    C. larvae

Answer key on page 32.

Glossary

bacteria
Tiny living things that can be either useful or harmful.

climate change
A human-caused global crisis involving long-term changes in Earth's temperature and weather patterns.

ecosystems
The collections of living things in different natural areas.

greenhouse gases
Gases in the air that trap heat from the sun.

larvae
Insects that have hatched from eggs and are in the early stages of life.

mandibles
Jaws that extend from an insect's head.

nutrients
Substances that living things need to stay strong and healthy.

pupae
Insects in the stage where they change from larva to adult.

species
Groups of animals or plants that are alike and can breed with one another.

To Learn More

BOOKS

Jaycox, Jaclyn. *Unusual Life Cycles of Invertebrates.* North Mankato, MN: Capstone Publishing, 2021.

Labrecque, Ellen. *Why Do Flies Like Gross Stuff?: Answering Kids' Questions.* North Mankato, MN: Capstone Publishing, 2021.

Rosenberg, Pam. *Gross Stuff Underground.* Mankato, MN: The Child's World, 2021.

NOTE TO EDUCATORS

Visit **www.focusreaders.com** to find lesson plans, activities, links, and other resources related to this title.

Index

B
bacteria, 18, 22, 24–25
beetles, 10–13, 22, 26

C
climate change, 24, 26
consumers, 9, 16

D
decomposers, 9, 16, 18, 26

E
ecosystems, 9, 15, 17, 24, 26
eggs, 5–7, 11–12

F
flies, 5–7, 10, 12, 26
fungi, 18, 21

G
greenhouse gases, 24
grubs, 10–11, 13, 19

H
humus, 17–19

L
leaf litter, 15, 18

M
maggots, 10, 12, 19
mandibles, 13

N
nutrients, 16–19, 21, 23, 25

P
producers, 9
pupae, 7, 10

T
tunnels, 10–11